# NIGERIAN ELECTIONS IN HISTORICAL PERSPECTIVE

Edited by
**B. Olatunji Oloruntimehin**

*Occasional Publication*
*Number 10*

*Published by*
**The Nigerian Academy of Letters**
Faculty of Arts, University of Ibadan
Ibadan, Nigeria

ISBN-13: 978-1535287340

ISBN-10: 1535287349

Frist Published in August, 2012

# Notes on Contributors

— Professor Ben Elugbe is the President of the Academy.

— Professor Segun Odunuga, the pioneer Secretary, is a past President of the Academy. His speech was delivered at the Fellows' Night in 2011.

— Professor B. Olatunji Oloruntimehin is the General Editor! Chairman, Publications Committee of the Academy.

— Professor Akinjide Osuntokun is currently at the Redeemer's University, Redemption City where he is Dean, College of Humanities. He delivered the Convocation Lecture in 2011.

## Table of Contents

# Preface

The Academy chose to deliberate on the subject of elections because elections are a crucial means of choosing individuals who could legitimately be Society's representatives in the processes of managing the affairs of the nation. Democratic governance is an arrangement in which Society or the people own the government of the nation- state and in which the government acts on behalf of, and for the people. Democracy is people-centred.

In Nigeria, as in many other parts of Africa, democracy has had a chequered history, and remains fragile. Part of the explanation has been that dominant political forces constantly undermine the effective involvement of the people as key players in the processes of governance. 'Nigerian Elections in Historical Perspective' seeks to find explanations to the problems of unrepresentative governments resulting in poor governance and retardation of economic and social development.

Of the three papers commissioned for presentation, only Professor Akinjide Osuntokun's Convocation Lecture is available. The balanced picture that the Academy had hoped for could therefore not be achieved. The introduction, *"Weighing Issues of Governance through Nigerian Elections in Historical Perspectives"* is aimed at providing some balance in the treatment of the subject.

Professor Segun Odunuga's speech is published to give members of the Academy and other readers a valuable insight into the stages of development of the Academy so far.

**B. Olatunji Oloruntimehin, FHSN, FNAL**

*General Editor*

# AN ADDRESS BY THE PRESIDENT OF THE NIGERIAN ACADEMY OF LETTERS (NAL) PROFESSOR BEN ELUGBE, ON THE OCCASION OF THE 13TH CONVOCATION AND THE INVESTITURE OF NEW FELLOWS OF THE ACADEMY IN LAGOS ON THE 11TH OF AUGUST, 2011

On behalf of the Nigerian Academy of Letters (NAL), I warmly welcome you to the 13th Convocation and the Ceremony of the Investiture of New Fellows of the Academy. Although some of us here are not members of the Academy, there is no doubt that the success of our gathering is insured by your presence. Whether of masquerades in our ancient communities, or of events such as the public inauguration of Presidents of countries, or of religious crusades, or of great sports events, the audience is of great importance. The audience, as my predecessor on this chair pointed out in 2009, is the matching essential, the indispensable participator.

Although I was elected President of the Academy a year ago, this is my first address to the Convocation of the Academy.

I was obviously very elated at the installation, a year ago, as the President of the Academy, and I thank my colleagues in the Academy for putting me in this exalted position.

Followers of our Convocations know that it is not usually an occasion for long Presidential addresses. And, with the prospect of an exciting convocation Lecture in a few minutes, I will not take too much of 'our time on this address.

All organisations, whether owned by government or independent, as in our case, face an eternal question of relevance and contribution. The first problem in this question, as far as the Academy is concerned, is that a sick person has to ask a doctor for help before the doctor can prescribe medication for their ailment. Moreover, in the prevailing atmosphere in our country, with people looking to see how they can get what they consider *their* share (fair or not) of the so-called "National Cake", an organization such as NAL, which has a high sense of integrity and self-respect, cannot afford to behave in a way that would make people think that it, too, is after its own share (fair or unfair) of the Cake. Therefore, although NAL is aware of its responsibility, it also knows that it must be sensible in trying to be of help.

For the avoidance of doubt, the Nigerian Academy of Letters, as the apex academic organization in the Humanities in Nigeria, is in a position to offer advice and service on all kinds of issues in this country. And we are not short on initiative and activity: we have regular *Occasional Publication* series and the less regular one *The Annals*. These organs of the Academy publish Annual

Lectures, Convocation Lectures, and papers from Scientific Sessions of the Convocation.

Every year, the Academy tries to reflect a theme that is current in national affairs. For example, last year was the jubilee anniversary of Nigeria's independence. Our theme was 'Fifty Years of Humanistic Studies in Nigeria'. This year's is 'Nigerian Elections in Historical Perspective'. The currency of the themes is not necessarily as visible or direct as these last two that I have just mentioned. However, even our biggest critics cannot deny the relevance and/or currency of themes such as 'Governance and Materialism', 'Public Morality', the 'Nigerian Ideal', etc. We are a non-profit organization. We are open to the scrutiny of the world, especially through our new website at *www.nalnigeria.org*. The site is very young — it was opened this year — and we invite our guests and our members to visit it on a regular basis.

We are also not an organisation of just words or 'hot air': we have awarded research fellowships of a post-doctoral sort to young scholars who are not members of the Academy. These fellowships are named after Chief Bayo Kuku, the Ogbeni Oja of Ijebu Land, who funds them. Some years ago, we held our Annual Lecture at the University of Port Harcourt and we received a donation of Five Million Naira from the River State Government, under the governorship of Chief Odili. We treat such donations as endowments, committed to one of our causes. Recently, Aihaji Adebola Adegunwa of the *Fototech* fame, also donated Five Million Naira and we have taken an initial decision as to what it will sponsor in our programmes. And I acknowledge, as well, donations of One Million Naira each from Lagos State, under Governor Babatunde Fashola, from Ondo under Governor Olusegun Mimiko, and from Edo, five hundred thousand naira (N500,000) under Governor Lucky Igbinedion. Other individuals have donated to our cause, and we are grateful to them all. Our faithful members continue to support the Academy with annual dues of Five Thousand Naira each. We are grateful of their membership and support.

My job is to ensure that the Academy remains focused on its ideals, comparable to what academies do elsewhere in the world. The election and investiture of Academic and Honorary Fellows is a part of that ideal because it enables us to recognize and reward, in our own small way, excellence in academics as well as in service to Nigeria. Our Academic Fellowships are open to professors of at least ten years standing while our Honorary Fellowships al-c open to all Nigerians who hold degrees in Humanities (or Arts). We also have Overseas Fellowships for Humanities academics abroad. In the case of academic or regular Fellowships, we only require that one be recommended or nominated by a fellow academic in one's discipline (not necessarily a Fellow, but a member), who is in a position to.. convince both our Screening Committee (invariably chaired by our Vice-

President) and our College of Fellows (COF) that one is ready for election as a Fellow. In the case of the Honorary Fellowships, NAL does not require the intervention of the COE The Executive Committee of the Academy receives and takes a decision on nominations to this category. The Executive Committee must be convinced that the nominee has contributed to society in a positive way.

Sometimes, it may appear to those outside that the basis for an Honorary Fellowship is unclear, but it is always clear to us. Last year, Dr. Uwaifo, better known to the public as a musician, was inducted into the Academy as an Honorary Fellow. Only the citation revealed to the public that Uwaifo was deserving of that honour. This year, Dr. Reuben Abati was elected an Honorary Fellow. After his election, he was given a job or responsibility at Aso Rock. That has nothing to do with his election, although we rejoice with Dr. Abati.

Our Convocation is invariably at the University of Lagos; but our Annual Lecture moves round the universities across the country. The University of Lagos has given us accommodation for administrative and other activities of the Academy at Number 8b, Ransome Kuti Road, on its campus. The current Vice-Chancellor of the University of Ibadan, Professor Isaac Adewole, has promised to provide a suitable building for our national headquarters at Ibadan. We are ever grateful to both universities.

This year's theme is 'Nigerian Elections in Historical Perspective'. The title that our Convocation Lecturer has chosen is 'Nigeria and the curse of elections'. It is obvious that this is a current and apt theme for this year in which elections have taken place. The Lecturer's view that elections in Nigeria are cursed will not land him in court — I don't think — hut this Emeritus Professor from the University of Lagos is best placed to take us on an excursion into the curse of Nigerian elections.

Our nation is a lucky one, loved by the Almighty. Those problems that lead to conflagrations in other African countries somehow find peaceful, if *quazi*, resolution here. But such resolutions invariably come at an unnecessary and avoidable cost to life and property. There is also the quiet cost that may not always be visible to, or understood by, the public: NAL's ability to move its activities round the country, for example, is adversely affected. Economic activities are stalled in those parts of the country where violence has taken place. NAL exists for and is committed to the peace and survival of the country. Therefore, we join all well-meaning Nigerians in condemning violence.

Allow me to thank you again for your presence and I hope that you will find your time with us rewarding, as I call on our famous Convocation Lecturer to deliver his lecture.

# THE CHALLENGES BEFORE NAL
## *Segun Odunuga*

The Nigeria Academy of Letters (NAL) has come to stay after f the initial teething problems that usually confront new a organisations. There ,was the doubt that our acronym, NAL, could c get confused with that of the Nigeria Assurance Limited which led to the suggestion by Professor JE Clark, in the first Academy Lecture — *A Peculiar Faculty* — that it might be better to adopt "the fuller ( name of Nigerian Academy of Arts and Letters (NAAL) to faithfully reflect our component faculties" Today, that fear has totally disappeared as neither the insurance company nor the NAL Merchant Bank is in contention with us over the acronym. In fact, NAL rings an academic bell in many circles since we went public in 1996.

All this while the Academy had only protem officers and this was the situation when in 1998 the Academy had its second lecture — *Myth, History and National Orientation in Nigeria* — delivered by Professor A.E. Afigbo and its first elections. At that point in our development we were still very conscious of the provisions of the Constitution, particularly those that have to do with changes therein. Articles 16 — Amendments — states clearly:

> *This Constitution may be amended at the Annual General Meeting of the Academy provided that:*

*a(i)*    *notice of such proposed amendments is received by the Secretary at least two month is to the date of the meeting.*

*a(ii)*   *two — thirds of those present at the Annual General Meeting vote in favour of such an amendment.*

*b.*    *The Secretary shall forward all notices of amendment to the members at least one month before the Annual General Meeting.*

Despite the fact that the Foundation President and the Secretary saw each other virtually on daily basis this provision was strictly followed and members at the AGM debated and passed those acceptable to them. Today, not many of us remember that our first constitution made provision for 1st and 2nd Vice Presidents. As we progressed it was thought that a 2nd Vice President would spend six years in the Presidency, so we amended the constitution at the AGM of August 11, 2000 to make room for only one. The intentment was that since the Vice President would automatically succeed the President a total of four years was enough. It was at that same AGM that we limited the President to a term of two years only and we also approved the establishment of the College of Fellows. But in 2004 we violated among other things that provision by rushing through without due process an amendment which aimed at. preventing the Vice President from automatically succeeding the President. The pretext was that some senior people might want to be President senior people who have not been active and are unfamiliar with the working system of the Academy. It was an unconstitutional move and invalid in law. Fortunately, at the next election no senior people tried to contest the post of President, and the Vice President thereby succeeded the President though he was denied the honour of being publicly presented at the Convocation as the incoming President. Since then things have returned to normal and the Vice President automatically succeeds the President.

At the College of Fellows held on June 18, 2004 Fellows reviewed the cost of bringing members to meetings and we adopted the use of electronic mail to reduce expenses. Today we have gone further than that in that we now vote electronically, though I must confess that the anxiety and excitement that characterized previous elections have disappeared. With this out of the way our AGM should be shorter. We should finish the business of the day faster.

At the meeting of the CollegOf Fellows in Ibadan on Friday, June 4, 2010 the issue of automatic fellowship for winners of' the NNOM ca was raised; but the status quo ante was maintained. The College of Fellows had decided on May 30, 2002: that The *Nigeria National Merit Order or any award far that matter of similar status should be regarded U as an asset but by no means an automatic guarantee of election as a Fellow in of the Nigeria*

15

*Academy of Letters.* There has been no departure from this decision.

Because of our decision that the Academy should not limit its activities to the South West re decided to hold our 2001 Annual Lecture in Jos. Thanks largely to the efforts of Professor Godwin Tasie who was the Chairman of the LOG we had a successful outing and the following year we were in Port Harcourt where we had a very beautiful time. It was Professor Tasie who gave the Annual Lecture and I must state that our own Professor Ayo Banjo was the then Pro-Chancellor of the University of Port Harcourt and he naturally ensured that things took proper shape. Since then we have been to different parts of the country — Benin, Kano, Nsukka, and Ekopma, Akungba and Ilorin, in 2012. In spite of all this, some all distinguished Nigerians that we have honoured complained of not d knowing anything about NAL until we approached them. We have to do more than present papers at Convocations and scientific sessions which are limited to our members. The Academy has Learned Societies in its fold and Faculties of Arts are expected to be our t institutional members. I have always advocated the need to organize joint activities with them. In showing our concern about the c declining patronage of some of the disciplines in the educational system, NAL devoted one convocation to considering the theme I "Who is afraid of History?" The Academy obviously will have to focus also on English in view of the falling standard of competence in all tiers of our educational system. Of course, other disciplines like Foreign or European Studies have not attracted our attention. We should change and collaborate with those recognized institutions that we count worthy of our attention. I believe the NAL can organize workshops, seminars and other activities in which non-members can participate in order to help improve disciplines in the humanities.

And that was the challenge placed before us at first Convocation Lecture held at the Nigerian Institute of International Affairs, Lagos, in 1999 when the Lecturer, Professor J.F. Ade-Ajayi stressed the fact that

> ...we chose the latter Academy not in the sense of Belles Lettres, or creative writing for aesthetic value only, but in the sense of men and women of Letters, people of culture, learning, erudition and knowledge committed to promoting their relevance to national development.

He also emphasized *the need to redress the science-Arts imbalance, to get resources for the human disciplines and to show that science and arts are interrelated and mutually interdependent.*

The Academy of Letters has in the past eleven (11) years taken up the challenge and as much as possible addressed issues of national importance at our convocation and scientific sessions. We have demonstrated our preparedness to collaborate with other Academies,

17

particularly Science and Social Science, to advance knowledge and contribute to national development. It is, undoubtedly, in recognition of this that the NNLG assigned to the Nigerian Academy of Letters the duty of searching for eminent Nigerians in the humanities while Science was given a similar task. My belief is that the Humanities cover Education, Social Science and Law as human disciplines. In a number of countries there is only one Academy of Arts and Science; but here we believe in the proliferation of Academies. In fact, one of us a few years ago attempted to float an Academy of Biblical Studies and I had to call the attention of Professor S.O. Abogunrinto this and he quickly nipped the move in the bud.

It is intriguing to note that we hold scientific sessions after our convocations because we put research into whatever we do. There is the debate about where to draw the line between science and the humanities, and some scholars attempt to examine two cultures in relation to them. Is there really a two-culture split between science and the humanities? As Ade-Ajayi pointed out, the humanities and the sciences are interrelated. We cannot say that one is concerned with values and meaning and the other with natural phenomena where one can put aside concerns of value and meaning.

As part of our activities to celebrate our fiftieth national independence anniversary, the Academy chose the theme: Fifty Years of *Humanistic Studies in Nigeria.*

How have we fared as an organization? Have we been able to look beyond Arts in our activities to demonstrate that indeed we are the apex organization in the humanities? Do we feel that any scholar, professional or person of culture with no degree in Arts deserves our attention?

Admittedly, NAL has on its own recognised the need to give leadership in getting the humanities acknowledged and respected. In doing so, NAL attempted to establish the Humanities Prize that would give the winner ₦ 1million. We were to have a seed fund of ₦20 million but we got scared because we relied on some sources that the then political terrain made slippery. That fright left our sister organization — Science Academy — having the ears of the Federal Government where it is believed that the scientists and their research are of great utility and greater significance. The Academy of Letters should challenge this. We know Nigeria is in the same situation as some countries. But we could learn from experiences of other nations. For example, in the United States of America, the National Science Foundation (NSF) for decades enjoyed government patronage particularly after the Russians launched the Sputnik in 1957. But the limitation inherent in focusing only on the sciences for national development was realized. To redress the situation the National Endowment for the Humanities was established in 1985 under sponsorship from scholars, educationists and politicians. Since then, many States have established their own Humanities Councils. We have looked too much in the direction of the Federal Government in Nigeria, forgetting that there are in the States Councils of Arts and Culture that we can work with. And there are 36 states. In fact, there is nothing wrong in our organizing a national council to create the awareness in the humanities. We have a long list of people in the humanities who would gladly join us in this endeavour. We only have to take the initiative. On the national level NAL can raise N20 million that scared us some years back.

I have read about the Texas Council on the Humanities directing that a project on *Science and Human Values* be initiated while the state of Maine counterpart launched a project on *Literature & Medicine: Humanities at the Heart of Health Care*. One family physician who participated was quoted as saying, we use literature to help strip away the assumptions we bring to work, and improve our understanding of our patients and each other.

I believe that there cannot be culture split between science and humanities. Does science, after all, not have cultural context?

We should be at the vanguard of the humanities galvanizing resources to make the disciplines relevant to socio-cultural, educational and moral development. We can do it and I know we have the leadership instinct in us to achieve this lofty national goal. It is a challenge we would face and make success of.

# WEIGHING ISSUES OF GOVERNANCE THROUGH NIGERIAN ELECTIONS IN HISTORICAL PERSPECTIVE

## *B. Olatunji Oloruntimehin*

Nigeria was fifty years old as an independent nation-state in 2010. The year 2011 was one of general elections — to the Presidency and National Assembly; and to State governorship and State Assemblies. It is generally known that Nigeria had endured almost forty years of military dictatorship out of her fifty years of post- colonial existence. With prolonged military rule, the nation experienced severe withering of her short legacy of democratic governance. Colonial rule, being alien rule, was understandably not about growing democratic institutions. The politics of decolonization leading to granting of independence also left its own negative mark on the structure of the post-colonial state and the orientation of politics in the country.

It is also correct to observe that military governments often operate, to all intents and purposes, as indigeneous colonial regimes. Prolonged military rule was destructive of the fledgling democratic institutions and practices, which began with the processes of attaining independence. From being a colonial state to the present, most of the dominant state actors and politicians have been more concerned with developing a political architecture which could be controlled and exploited as an estate than as a nation-state, with a great diversity of nationalities that need to be integrated on the basis of shared values and commitment to people-centred socio-economic development.

Most of the dominant State actors have been obsessed with building a political system in which individuals convert institutions and official responsibilities to personal gain. For most of these actors, the principal concern has been in sustaining a prebendal state in which government is run as "eatery."

It has been rightly observed that Nigeria is hung by her history. 1-ler independence came through incremental constitutionalism, from Lord Lugard's amalgamation through several colonial administrations, and through prolonged military regimes of different hues. As Ayoade observed,

> ... *The Culture of Constitution mongering was established resulting in four Constitutions after the independence Constitution (1963, 1979, 1989 and 1999). The audacity of the military in assuming competence in writing constitutions for the people has contributed to this negative tradition. They even equate themselves with the people by plagiarizing other Constitutions with the preambles,*

'We, the people....'

*...A Constitution remains apiece of uncomfortable literature when its spirit does not emanate from the people, nor rooted in their hearts...*[2]

A Constitution, on the contrary, is normally a living document. Not having involved the people in the processes leading to the promulgation of the Constitution, it has been a hard task grafting it into the consciousness of the people, and having the people accept it as their definition as a people of one nation, with a supposedly shared future. Patriotism is normally an expression of shared nationalism. Nationalism is also a consciousness on the part of individuals or groups, of membership in a nation, or of a desire to promote the strength, liberty or prosperity of a nation. The constant clamour for national conferences (Sovereign or not) is an expression of the alienation between state and society.

The transition of power from the last military regime to Civilian rule in 1999 was precipitated by the necessity to avert the threatening disintegration of the country as a nation — state. The instability of regimes that resulted from long years of ruling over, and not with, the people had become a threat to the survival of the state. Nigeria has become a perfect illustration of the alienation of the people from the state.

Although the withdrawal of the Military from the suffocating domination of national life brought relief to the politically articulate among the citizenry, the hope that the country would recover, and re-establish itself as a democracy has remained largely elusive. The new civilian regime was constructed upon a false foundation with a constitution which the military imposed on the people. The 1999 Constitution created a nation-state with the character of a living lie or delusion. The preamble to the Constitution makes the false claim that WE THE PEOPLE *of the Federal Republic of Nigeria give* it to ourselves. It has been observed, variously, that the preamble lies about both the constitution and the people of Nigeria.

It is an empirical fact that the crises of governance which confound Africa's economic and social development can in fact be attributed to the failure of African rulers to forge symmetry between the power of the State and that of the people. Nigeria exemplifies the crises. Nigerian citizens clamour for democratic governance as an antidote' to national decay. Democratic governance has become the political right of people all over the world. It is the means by which people, as citizens, can own their government. Governments which result from the democratic process engage in mutual dialogue with the people who have proprietary rights over the government. It is this kind of relationship that ensures a harmonious transaction within the state. Democracy is anchored upon the will of the people which, according to the Universal Declaration of Human Rights, shall be the basis of authority of government. In a democracy, Government is the agent and not the principal of the people. In constructing and running such a government, elections are a crucial force.

Elections are a means of gauging the level of civic liberties, human rights and freedom, especially freedom of choice and expression that is available to individual citizens and groups within the polity. Elections in a democracy involve meaningful and extensive competition among individuals and recognized groups (especially political parties) for all effective positions of government power, at regular intervals, and without the use of force or violence. Elections are a means of establishing a highly inclusive level of political participation in the selection of leaders and policies. Elections are founded upon the existence of a vibrant level of civil and political liberties (freedom of expression, freedom of the press or communication media, freedom to form and join political associations and organisations) sufficient to ensure the integrity of political competition and participation[3]

For elections to play their roles as expressions of the will of the people, they must be free and fair. Conducting free and fair elections has been the greatest problem that bedevils Nigeria's political scene and socio-political development.

The elections which produced the civilian regime that succeeded the military in 1999 were flawed. But subsequent ones in 2003, 2007, notably were considerably worse. They were glaringly rigged under the direction of a

President who believed that politics and elections arc other forms of war.

Nigeria's experience of governance since 1999 has been largely that of a movement towards despotism. Democratic institutions which are prescribed in the military imposed Constitution have been assiduously subverted in the process of promoting the interests of a cabal, and/or a political collectivity which shares nothing or little of the norms or practice of democratic governance. Indeed, the eight- year rule of General (Chief) Olusegun Obasanjo, an erstwhile military Head of State, witnessed considerable attenuation of the role and relevance of the *people* in the processes of governance. As expected reactions were also building up against this negative trend.

...Since 1999, electioneering has been conducted as war to be won at all costs (*'do or die'*) to maintain a cabal that operates as an oligopoly, whose main concern is to run the Nigerian State as its estate. The struggle seems to be aimed at turning Nigeria into a one-party state to gratify the cabal's greed for power and wealth. The result of this orientation and approach has been the denudation of national institutions and values that could make people identify with the nation-state. Elections have been turned into the means of achieving the goals of a cabal, which uses agencies of state, especially security forces, for its own goals.

The Nigerian Academy of Letters (NAL) chose to consider the subject of *Nigerian Elections in Historical Perspective* at its annual Convocation in 2011 because elections are a critical part of the processes of the evolution and sustenance of governments in modern democracies. Secondly, given the political history of Nigeria, the choice of subject was to provide a barometer for assessing what progress is being made in integrating the diverse political communities in Nigeria with the Nigerian state that has hitherto operated as an imposed superstructure.

Elections are crucial to the realization and sustainability, not only of the idea, but reality of government being of the people.

The choice of Nigeria Elections in Historical Perspective as our subject of consideration in 2011 was also in continuation of our Academy's concern for the promotion of good governance as the bedrock of human society. The Academy is concerned that Man in society be the template of good governance. It is a truism that

*...where man ceases to be the goal and means of governance (and with it politics) there seems to be a short passage to lawlessness, and escalation of violence and counter-terror, from any quarter in society and the state...*[4]

The Academy had addressed and published on aspects of the problem such works *as Language and Good governance*, History, *Morality and Public Order, The Wages of Obsessive Materialism and The Humanities and Good governance.*

Three scholars were commissioned to make presentations at the 2011 Convocation. Professor Akinjide Osuntokun's *Nigeria and The Curse of Elections* was the Convocation Lecture. A careful reading of the lecture will provide a valuable insight into the explanations for the tottering state of the Nigerian nation-state, and some good illustrations for issues raised in this introduction.

The Curse of Elections is an expression of the denial of the Rule of Law, and imposition of force by divers means.

Where governments are constituted and run in denial of the rights of individuals in society to enjoy freedom from threat to life, liberty, especially to choose in free and fair elections, between competing ideologies and political actors, the states run through such governments are undermined.

As a prominent Nigerian lawyer put it, when comparing the experience of the United States of America with Nigeria's, Nigeria is ... '*A Country in search of a birth certificate*'. As he observes...

> ... *we have been transiting, on an experimental basis, with one constitution after the other all of*

*them initiated and propelled by the military and militarism.., all attempting to build a superstructure on the quicksand of the duo of Mr. & Mrs. Lugard...*[5]

Along all these is the corresponding decay of edifying virtues such as loyalty to nation.

As Hugh Seton-Watson observed, ....

*Nationalism (patriotism) speaks and acts on behalf of the nation. What is the nation?... a nation exists when an active and fairly numerous section of its members are convinced that it exists..., when they have mass support, and in the process of the emergence of mass support economic and social forces play a tremendously important part. But nationalism cannot even begin until there is an* elite of convinced nationalists, expressing the national idea, and this cannot happen until a national consciousness has been formed.

The concern here is with consciousness on the part of individuals or groups of membership in a nation, or of a desire to forward the strength, liberty or prosperity of a nation.

Contemporary events in Nigeria present the stark consequence of ruling over and not with people. We are witnesses to the phenomena of a failing or disintegrating state, anarchy, and collapse of cultures as embodied in values such as respect for life, human dignity, excessive materialism and pandemic corruption.

It is apt to warn that …

> *no society can live and function under the constant obsession of its own impending dissolution: the hypothesis of survival must be accepted, faith in the possibility of survival must exist, in order that Society may be able to live and work for it...*[7]

## Notes

1. Wale Adebanwi (2010), A Paradise For Maggots: *The Story of A Nigerian Anti-Graft Czar*. (Published in Nigeria); Bamidele A. Sohowale (2011) PDP *Corruption Incorporated, Ibadan*, AIKE Books.
2. J.A.A. Ayoade (2010), *Nigeria: Positive Pessimism and Negative Optimism A Valedicto7y Lecture*. Faculty of the Social Sciences, University of Ibadan, September 17, 2101, pp. 19-20.
3. B. Olatunji Oloruntimehin (2009), Man in Society as Template of Good Governance in *The Humanities And Good Governance*, NAL *Occasional* Publication, No. 6, p. 26.
4. Tekena N. Tamuno (2011), 'Scholars, Society and the State: Their Challenges And Responses Concerning Nation-Building in Nigeria?,' 3rd Convocation

Lecture, Bells University of Technology, Ota, Nigeria, Friday, 4th November, 2011, p.27

5. Wole Olanipekun (2012) Nigeria: "A Country in Search of a Birth Certificate" in *The Nation*, Tuesday, June 5, 2012, p.46.

6. Hugh Seton-Watson (1965) *Nationalism Old and New*, Sydney University Press, pp.3, 12-13; Royal Institute of International Affairs, (1939), *Nationalism*, London.

7. Edward Hallett Carr (1960), The New society, London, Macmillan & Co Ltd., p.100.

## Some References

M. Chris Alli (2001), *The Federal Republic of Nigeria: The Siege of a Nation*. Ikeja, Malthouse Press Ltd.

Babafemi A. Badejo (2008) *Politicization of Ethnicity, Inequities and Electoral Violence in Kenya*, Lagos, CBAAC Occasional Monograph, No. 9.

Jean-Francois *Bayartet al* (1999) *The Criminalization of the State in Africa*, Bloomington, Indiana University Press.

L. Diamond (1995), 'Nigeria: *The Uncivic Society and Descent into Praetorianism'* in *Diamond, L., Lintz, J* and Lipset S. (eds). *Politics in Developing Countries: Comparing Experiences with Democracy*. Boulder: Lynn Rienner Publishers.

Richard Joseph (1996), 'Nigeria Inside the Dismal Tunnel," Current History, May 1996.

Richard Joseph (1991), *Democracy and Prebendal Politics in Nigeria.' The Rise and fall of the Second Republic*, Ibadan, Spectrum Books.

John Stuart Mill (1859) *On Liberty*, London and Felling—on-Tynn, New York and Melbourne. (with an Introduction by WL. Courtney) London, July 1901 (Kinde Edition, 2011, Amazon .com).

B. Olatunji Oloruntimehin (2007), *Culture and Democracy*, Lagos, CBAAC Occasional Monograph, No. 5.

B. Olatunji Oloruntimehin (2001), 'State-owned Enterprises and Corruption in Nigeria' in *African Journal of Public Administration and Management* vol. xiii, Nos. 1&2, January and July 2001.

Renate Zahar (1969) (tr. by Willfried F. Feuser (1974) *Colonialism and Alienation, Concerning Frantz Fanon's Political Theory*, Benin City, Ethiope Publishing Corporation.

# NIGERIA AND THE CURSE OF ELECTIONS

**Professor Akinjide Osuntokun:** *OON, FNAL*
**Dean, College of Humanities**
**Redeemer's University**
**Redemption Camp**
**josuntokun@yahoo.com**

## Introduction

Holding of periodic elections is central to democratic governance. Universal suffrage is however relatively new in the long march of democracy from its ancient Athenian roots of direct democracy to the current global practice of representative government. Suffrage in Athenian democracy was in no way universal, it was in fact restricted to citizens and adult males since rights went with responsibility of military service in most of the                Greecian States. Slaves and foreigners were of course barred from city meetings. Whatever its limitation, the Athenian model provided an example of how government should not be the dictate of one person or a group of persons no matter how prepared for it. They may of course be well prepared asplato in his **Republic** had tried to argue that democracy was not the ideal form of government. Rather he preferred a system of specialised training and intellectual preparation of the ruling class or ideally of an all knowing philosopher king. This specialisation is however embedded in the highly professional civil service characteristic of modern

States. Europe of the age of the enlightenment tried this idea of philosopher kings when enlightened despotism prevailed in France, the German and Italian States as well as in the Hapsburg Empire centred on Vienna. The French revolution and its revolutionary ideas of the rights of man and the citizen presaged the advent of representative democracy in Europe as a whole. The story is slightly different in the Anglo- Saxon world of the British and the American who can rightly claim to be the homeland or fountain of Representative Democracy. Democracy as we know it today owes its development to Western liberal idea of fundamental human rights which are inherent in all human beings in the sense that they are the birthright of all men. These rights are also inalienable and cannot be given up nor can people be denied them. They are also universal since they apply to all regardless of nationality, gender status or race. This liberal idea is captured in the American Declaration of Independence in, 1776 which among other things said:

> *"We take these truths to be self evident, that all men are created equal and that they are endowed by their creator with certain inalienable rights, that amongst these are the rights to life, liberty and the pursuit of happiness..."*

The British even as far back as the time of the *Magna Carta* (1215) and the Bill of Rights (1689) had struggled with their Kings to demand for rule of law and respect for the rights of the individual. Some form of representation and even elections however limited, had held in England from the 17th Century. The franchise was limited and in the United States of Thomas Jefferson, Benjamin Franklin and George Washington, the franchise was restricted to property owners, slavery was legal in spite of their revolutionary pretensions. England until 1832 so-called "Great Reform Bill" was the home of pocket and rotten boroughs which rich people in the cities, particularly in London could buy and from which they became members of Parliament without any election. Even the Great Reform Bill of 1832 did not go far enough and universal adult suffrage including the right of women to vote did riot come until the election of 1918 after the First World War and women were given the vote on the grounds that their war service deserved to he rewarded. This preamble is necessary to briefly state that universal representative Democracy is relatively recent in the long political history of man.

## NIGERIA AND RPRFSINTATIVE DEMOCRACY

Representative Democracy for any part of Nigeria was stridently demanded for by the Western educated elite who felt marginalized and ignored during the Governor-Generalship of Sir Fredrick Lugard. In one of the first salvos in favour of electoral system, one of the organs of the educated elite argued that, under Representative government

*"....The fatuous eccentricities of the present administration.., would never be. Any administration absurdly harassing the peace and destroying the good will, harmony of the community and people would soon through popularly elected council know the relationship of ruler and subject..."*

Under Representative government it went on to say"

*...All privileges that are due to the ruler will be swept away, social lines of demarcation between classes will be less sharply defined. Economy will replace extravagance in public departments. Sinecures and excessive salaries will no longer exist. Africa will be rid of all exotics and foreign imposters."*[1]

Lugard was naturally dismissive of the educated Nigerians who were said to represent no one except themselves. Lugard in dismissing their call for Representative government had said among other things that:

*"...There is the chronic and abiding trouble of secret sedition and disloyalty of Lagos... They are masters of secret intrigue and they have been plotting against the government ceaselessly. I could show you that Lagos has for 20 years past opposed every governor and has formented strife and bloodshed in the hinterland....After nearly 12 years as Governor here, I am free to say that the people of Lagos* are the lowest, the most

seditious and disloyal, the most prompted by purely self seeking money activities of any people I have ever met."[2]

The recrimination and mutual hatred or dislike can be seen when the editor of Lagos Weekly Record on the 5th of October 1918 wrote calling for a

*"Free Africa" That " will no longer be exploited by a ruling caste of European overlords and that the government of the people and for the people shall be the rule in Africa as in Europe, nor can self government be longer denied certain peoples upon*

the fantastic pretext that there are superior and inferior people."[3]

Lugard was not predisposed to call for elections in Nigeria because he rightly felt that the educated Nigerians on the coast did not represent all Nigerians and furthermore, even if he were to offer them electoral representation, they would be hopelessly divided among themselves.

It was no surprise that the more liberal Governor-General Sir Hugh Clifford who replaced Lugard was more sympathetic to educated Africans and their demand for elections into the Legislative Council in Lagos. Hugh Clifford abolished the "Nigerian Council" described by the educated elite as a mere talking shop made up of colonial officials and Oba Ladigbolu, the Alaafin of Oyo, Muhammad Abbas, Emir of Kano, and one Nana Dore, an

Itshekiri Chief from the Delta and Sir Kitoyi Ajasa as Representatives of the people. He replaced the Council with an elected Legislative Council. Even the Liberal Hugh Clifford sometimes dismissed the claims of educated Nigerians as representatives of the wider Nigerian society of uneducated peoples. Commenting on the formation of British West African Congress after the First World War he wrote;

*"There has during the last few months been a great deal of loose and gaseous talk....which has for most part emanated from a self- selected and self-appointed congregation of educated African gentlemen... It can only be described as farcical to suppose that...continental Nigeria can be represented by a handful of gentlemen drawn from a ha if dozen coast tribes — men born and bred in British administered towns situated on the seashore, who in the safety of British protection have peacefully pursued their studies under British teachers.....*

Sir Hugh went on in his address to the Legislative Council in Lagos in 1920 with a clincher to say that the educated Nigerians were separated by a wide chasm from their unlettered folks when he declared:

*"I will leave Honourable members to imagine what these gentlemen's experience would be, if instead of travelling peacefully to Liverpool in a British ship they could be deposited, unsustained by British*

*protection among.... The...cannibals of the Mama Hills. .. The determinedly naked warriors of the inner Ibo country, and there left to explain their claims to be recognised as the accredited representatives of these their fellow nationals*"[4]:

In spite of this limitation Hugh Clifford conceded four elected representatives to Nigerians in the Legislative Council elections in 1923 with three representing Lagos and one Calabar. Thus began the long journey of electoral politics in Nigeria. The Legislative Council was inaugurated in 1923. The political history of Lagos during the period 1923-1938 centred on the quinquennial elections for the Legislative Council and, the triennial elections for the Lagos town council. The elections were fought on the perennial question of the House of Docemo (Dosumu) and the Status of the Oba of Lagos. Electoral politics was dominated by Herbert Macaulay, founder of the Nigerian National Democractic Party (NNDP). Its candidates were victorious in the election of 1923, 1928, and 1933. This party remained the dominant force until 1938. The lone candidate from Calabar was elected on the platform of the Calabar Improvement League (CIL). One thing is clear and this is that elections were generally fair. If not, the British would have done everything to stop Herbert Macaulay's party from winning. Their leader had been jailed twice by the British for minor infractions of the law and they could have used this fact to outlaw his party. Furthermore, younger elements were becoming frustrated with Herbert Macaulay's obsession with the status of the Oba of Lagos to the detriment of what they considered much more fundamental such as the status of Nigeria itself. Although the party was most of the time seized with how to restore the Obaship of Lagos to its rightful place, by the 1930s branches of Macaulay's NNDP began to spring up especially in Yorubaland. Dr C.C. Adeniyi-Jones, the President of the party and one of its representatives in the Legislative Council from 1926 to 1938 began to raise issues that struck at the very basis British colonial rule in Nigeria. The fate of political parties was however tied to constitutional changes in Nigeria particularly after the Second World War. However, in the inter war years many currents of political nature had swept into Nigeria. The 1930s in particular witnessed the formation of the Nigerian Youth Movement formed by Samuel Akinsanya, Ernest Ikoli, Dr. J.C. Vaughn and Hezikiah Oladipo Davies in 1934. It was previously the Lagos Youth Movement until 1936. Gradually this movement challenged and eclipsed the older Nigerian National Democratic Party. The contest between the NNDP of Macaulay and the NYM of the younger people was marked by mutual recrimination and bitterness. The NYM was joined by Nnamdi Azikiwe, American educated journalist with degrees from Lincoln and Howard and higher degrees from Ivy League Universities of Columbia and Pennsylvania. Nnarndi Azikiwe was the first Igbo man in modern Nigeria to earn a degree from any University and he was thus seen by his people as their tribune and champion. He rose to the occasion by championing their cause by founding newspapers that eulogised their achievements and their credo of political republicanism. With the combination of Azikiwe and H.O. Davies who had newly        graduated from the London School of Economics as a lawyer the NYM became a potent force in Nigerian nationalism with branches far and wide in the country. The emphasis of political agitation for the first time shifted from Lagos issues to such an issue as the right price of Cocoa in 1938 following attempts to depress the producer price by some European monopolies in West Africa. The election of 1938 in which the NNDP was worsted was therefore fought on economic issues rather than on political issues of the Lagos Obaship institution. Of course embedded in the Cocoa crisis were larger issues of political economy of a dependent and peripheral colony in the British Empire. The solid consensus of political activists soon broke asunder in 1941 when there was a vacancy in the Lagos Legislative Council following the resignation from the Council by Dr. K.A. Abayomi on his appointment to the Governor-General's Executive Council. Two candidates from the NYM showed keen interest. One was Samuel Akinsanya foundation member of the NYM and Secretary General of Nigerian Motor Transport Union while the other was Ernest Ikoli, also a foundation     member and President of the NYM and editor of its press organ the *Daily Service*. The rank and file seemed to have favoured Akinsanya who was also          Azikiwe's candidate and was therefore supported by members of the Ibo National Union. Ernest Ikoli on the other hand was supported by the grandees of the NYM including the up and coming Ibadan based Obafemi Awolowo among others. There was no election and Ernest Ikoli by acclamation was returned as candidate of the NYM and he subsequently won the 1941 election. This led to schism within the NYM. Azikiwe accused his opponents of tribalism, and left the party followed by many including his Igbo compatriots. Samuel Akinsanya left politics entirely to become a traditional ruler in Isara as *Odemo*. This marked the beginning of bitterness in electoral politics in Nigeria and presaged the bitterness between Azikiwe and Awolowo in subsequent years. The Akinsanya crisis was the first major manifestation of tribal tension that affected all subsequent efforts to achieve unity in Nigeria. The crisis          was rather complex. Most of the established leaders of the nationalist movement in Lagos resented the brash American journalistic campaign of Azikiwe and  his *West African Pilot* and other regional papers of the same hue and orientation established by Azikiwe. Azikiwe's entry into  Lagos politics was seen as the attempt of a *par venu* upstart from nowhere taking over leadership of a movement whose provenance he knew little of. Akinsanya was also resented as an Ijebu against whom some other Yorubas nursed animus because of their formidable economic position astride the North-South trade route from which they had historically benefited. The electoral crisis of 1941 was therefore caused by a conjunction of latent and immediate reasons that were to have reverberation in electoral politics of Nigeria for a years to come. The result of the crisis was the destruction of the a NYM as a formidable force in Nigerian Politics as witnessed by the departure of Azikiwe from the NYM; H.O. Davies took a government appointment, as previously indicated Samuel Akinsanya became Odemo of Ishara and the NYM became moribund except for the Ibadan branch whose light flickered on under Obafemi Awolowo a minor produce buyer until 1943.

The war years saw the failure of several attempts to unite the various political movements, until the Nigerian Union of Students (NUS) formed in 1939 put pressure on leaders through mobilization of its members. The NUS called a Conference in August 1944 in Lagos of all organizations including the NYM which declined, for the purpose of organising a national council, to in their own words "weld the heterogeneous masses of Nigeria into one solid block." On August 26, 1944, the inaugural meeting of the conference was held and it resolved:

> *"Believing our country is rightfully entitled to liberty and prosperous life.... And determined to work in unity for the realization of our ultimate goal of selfgovernment within the British Europe, we hereby bind ourselves together forming the Nigerian National Council."*[5]

Herbert Macaulay was elected President and Nnamdi Azikiwe the General Secretary. This was not a political party but a rally of several organizations including even tribal unions. The name subsequently became National Council of Nigeria and the Cameroons (NCNC) because Cameroonian Associations in Lagos such as *Bamenda Improvement Association*, The Bakweri Union and the Cameroon Youth League joined the Council. The NCNC from 1944 to 1957 became the dominant political party in Nigeria. While this was going on, Awolowo had proceeded to the United Kingdom in 1944 to study law and had in 1947 written his seminal *book path to Nigerian Freedom* magisterially advocating the federal system of government as the only workable constitution for a country with the kind of ethnic and religious plurality of Nigeria. He returned to Nigeria to organise a political party the *Action Group* which took a contrary position to the NCNC's advocacy of a unitary form of government. The strength of the two political parties was first tested in 1951 and the acrimony surrounding events after the election has remained with us till today. The election into the newly created Western Region's House of Assembly was of historical significance partly because the two contending parties represented constrasting political thinking in that part of Nigeria. The NCNC then led by Dr. Nnamdi Azikiwe after the demise of Herbert Macaulay the doyen of Nigerian nationalism saw itself as a political rally of all Nigerians, a mass movement, some sort of political hurricane sweeping British colonialism out of the way. The NCNC also liked to feel that the ethnic differences of Nigerians did not matter and that over time these differences will disappear. The story is often told of how Dr. Nnamdi Azikiwe told Ahmadu Bello that Nigerians should forget their ethnic differences but Ahmadu Bello retorted that rather than forget their differences they should understand them. The Action Group under its leader Obafemi Awolowo felt the ethnic differences constituted fundamental questions which could only be tackled through a confederal structure in which the ethnic reality of Nigeria was appreciated and realistically dealt with and that no matter the pretensions that they did not exist these differences would not disappear. The 1951 elections into the three Regional Houses in Kaduna, Enugu and Ibadan was through carefully organised electoral colleges. The people as such were not voting directly for the candidates. The result of the election in the North saw the Northern People Congress (NPC) as the majority party. The NCNC easily won in the East but in the West where the A.G. emerged as winners the result was disputed. The NCNC claimed its members were bought over. What indeed happened was that considerable number of members of the House came in as independents and went with the emerging Action Group majority[6].. Dr. Nnamdi Azikiwe who had been elected from Lagos and had wanted to lead the government was therefore frustrated out of the West and he went to the East and ousted Professor Eyo

Ita who had emerged as the leader of the government. Thus, emerged the fissiparous tendencies and ethnic bifurcation of Southern Nigerian politics as well as ethnic bitterness between the Igbo and Yoruba political leadership up to the present time. When Obafemi Awolowo became Premier of the West the NCNC under Nnamdi *Azikiwe* who was Premier in Eastern Nigeria saw it as its bounden duty to undermine the Action Group government in the West. The acrimony and political hatred was equally reciprocated in the same degree and measure. The NCNC was so formidable in the West that it always gave the Action Group a run for its money. This was simply because the NCNC had been planted from 1944 in the hearts of the Yorubas particularly in the urban centres of Lagos, Ibadan, Ijebu-Ode, Shagamu, Abeokuta, Ilesha, Oshogbo, Akure, Ondo and Ado-Ekiti, and virtually in all urban centres in the country. It became quite difficult for the Action Group to dislodge the NCNC from the psyche of the Yoruba people. Furthermore the almost innate political liberality of the Yoruba was against the idea of a tribal party which was what to many the Action Group represented. All attempts to tar the NCNC with the brush of Igbo tribalism failed because quite a few of the NCNC big wigs were Yorubas like Adegoke Adelabu the "lion of Ibadan" T.O.S. Benson of Ikorodu, Adeleke Adedoyin, Scion of Shagamu Royal House, Babatunji Olowofoyeku and J.E Fadahunsi of Ijeshaland and a host of former members of the old NYM and NNDP who found their ways into the NCNC. Obafemi Awolowo's genius lay in the way he utilised, some would say, manipulated the Yoruba traditional institutions particularly the Obas to discreetly champion the cause of the Action Group. The government which he headed in 1951 was so well run that over time the A.G. received massive support from the rural areas and small towns and particularly from the agricultural community that benefited from enhanced commodity prices particularly the market price of cocoa. Even then this did not prevent the resurgence of the NCNC in the federal elections of 1954 when the Action Group, the governing party in the saddle at regional level was worsted in the federal elections in the West. The fairness of the election was so obvious that there was no dispute at all. The Action Group accepted the defeat without complaining and moved on to reorganise and restrategise for the future. This transparency was unfortunately a rarity in the electoral history of Nigeria. But it proved that the democratic practice of voting out and removing from power for whatever reasons, a ruling party, if the people so desire it is possible even in Nigeria.

Until 1947 the Northern part of Nigeria was not represented in the Legislative Council. The area was administered through the Indirect Rule System in which power was shared between the Emirs and British colonial administrators. The events in the South led to the emergence of cultural associations like the *Jam'iyyar*

*Mutanen Arewa.* This was to later become a political party in response to the Macpherson Constitution of 1951. The North actually wanted to be left alone and they were honest about this. In 1948, Mallarn Abubakar Tafawa Balewa who subsequently became Prime Minister of Nigeria said:

> *"Many Nigerians deceive themselves by thinking that Nigeria is one... This is wrong..."*[7]

In fact in the constitutional talks between 1949 and 1950 Northern leaders impliedly threatened secession if they were not granted.

Their demands, which they articulated as follows:

1.     No boundary adjustment between the North and South to favour the South.

2.     Representation in the Federal House of Representatives must be according to population and that the North must be and guaranteed 50 percent representation.

3.     Central Revenue should be shared on population basis. in its

The coming of the North into the main stream of Nigerian politics ft introduced a forceful element into the tripartite politics of Nigeria in which the North remained the fulcrum of power around which the others revolved. It did not matter what the North did or did not over do it was always on the winning side.

The history of Nigeria is clear on the fact that the North forced its the a way through in spite of whatever their compatriots in the South and wished. This was a classical case of tyranny of numbers! Real elections into the Regional Houses were held in the North and the West in 1956 with the NPC and the AG being returned with greater elect majorities, while election into the Eastern House was delayed until gain after the Foster-Sutton Commission of Enquiry which investigated dead Dr. Nnamdi Azikiwe's conduct in connection with the Affairs of Sir J the African Continental Bank which he founded and in which the 1957 finances of the Eastern Region were kept. The report published in January 1957 had said among other things that Azikiwe's conduct in connection with the Affairs of the bank fell short "of expectations of honest reasonable people. The crisis was however resolved Awo politically by the NCNC when it advised Azikiwe to transfer all his door rights and interests in the Bank to the government of Eastern Nigeria. Azikiwe in March 1957 sought a new electoral mandate. Although the NCNC was weakened by this scandal but it did not prevent the party from being in power in the Eastern Region as well as controlling the majority of Western parliamentarians in the federal legislative capital. It used this power to deny the Action Group its desire for Lagos merger with the West in the London Constitutional Conference of 1957.

The Federal election of 1959 on the eve of independence scheduled 1960 for 1st of October 1960 was fought with everything the three main political parties had. The NPC was not interested in fielding candidates in the South. Even though some elements in the Niger- Delta sought alliance with it, the NPC merely wanted to be left alone in its Northern redoubt. The A.G under Awolowo saw the Northern soft belly in the middle belt and even in the North Eastern part of Northern Nigeria. It also championed the cause of minorities in the Niger Delta and the Calabar-Ogoja part of Eastern Nigeria. The A.G was particularly well organised and primed for campaigns all over the country with aeroplanes and helicopters and sophisticated gargetry the like of which had never been seen in Nigeria. It forced the aristocratic leaders of the NPC to campaign in the dusty small and large towns of Northern Nigeria to its great discomfort and embarrassment. Allegation of voting and ballot stuffing within the confines of the palaces of the emirs were made after the A.G. lost the elections in the North. The NCNC kept hold of the East and made gains in the West but at the end of all the efforts the election was deadlocked and the British showing favours to the NPC, called on Sir Abubakar Tafawa Balewa who had been Prime Minister since 1957 to form a new government.[8]

This led to recriminations and futile attempt by the Southern political leaders to form alliance while each of them or elements of them were negotiating coalition agreements with the NPC. Obafemi Awolowo's attempt to serve tinder an Azikiwe led government was doomed from the beginning, because like an elephant Azikiwe never forgot what he called Awolowo's perfidy of 1951 rightly or wrongly. The Action Group grudgingly went into opposition blaming its electoral debacle on rigging in the North, an accusation which a renegade British colonial official later confirmed. Suffice it to say that the 1959 election foreshadowed the future of electoral malpractices in Nigeria. At least the restraining hands of British officials ensured some semblance of sanity in the conduct of elections up till the coming down of the Union Jack on 1 of October 1960.

## POST INDFPENDLNCE ELECTIONS

The next two elections, namely the federal elections of 1964 and the Western elections of 1965 marked the decline of electoral democracy in Nigeria. Between 1961 and 1962 political crisis broke out it Western Nigeria.[9] The best organised party in Nigeria, the Action Group suffered from internal collapse and external aggression. The fault line between Obafemi Awolowo, the party leader who had moved to the centre hoping to become the Prime Minister of the country but ended as disgruntled leader of opposition and his deputy Chief S.L.A. Akintola, who had replaced Awolowo as Premier of

Western Nigeria centred on control of the government of Western Nigeria. The question really was who was to control the government. Was it to be the party leader Chief Obafemi Awolowo or the Premier the head of government? In an identical situation in the NPC the Prime Minister Sir Abubakar Tafawa Balewa, who was deputy to Ahamadu Bello controlled his government. But this was because the Northern Premier had a full plate running the affairs of the Nod and he was largely not interested in the affairs of the federation sc long as the Northern interest was protected. In the case of Awolowo the situation was different. Awolowo was an energetic man who suddenly found himself out of limelight and out of power. Ht naturally championed the cause of party supremacy. Akintola or the other hand finding himself as head of government and not in power and not in control of some of his lieutenants especially those running public corporations in which the West had invested large sums of money, was resentful of Awolowo's long distance control and his being reduced to a puppet and figure head. The situation was then exploited by those supporting them sometimes for pecuniary and or political reasons. The situation was compounded by external forces represented by the NCNC and the NPC that wanted to destroy the Action Group partly because the party presented the two governing parties formidable challenges in their regions. All the latter day talk of the crisis arising as Akintola's refusal to embrace the new political ideology of democratic socialism of the Action Group was mere rationalisation. The upshot of this is that the party collapsed and all attempts to mend fences failed. The Action Group broke apart. Akintola after the fracas in the House of Assembly was manipulated back to power by federal might in coalition with the NCNC in the \Vest. By the time of the federal election of 1964, the Akintola led government of the West emerged with a new party the NNDP This party went into an alliance with the NPC forming a grand Alliance of the Nigerian National Alliance (NNA) while the remnants of the Action Group entered into an Alliance with its old enemy the NCNC to form the United Peoples Grand Alliance (UPGA). What was going to be a showdown of forces ended in a farce when the UPGA boycotted the election claiming electoral malpractices. This led to the NPC and NNDP forming a broad- based government with the NCNC at the centre. By this time the bitterness and tension in the West had reached a level of make or break, particularly since 1963 when Awolowo and his subordinates were jailed for treasonable felony. His supporters had hoped that the 1965 election in the West would afford them the opportunity to throw out the Akintola government. But this was not to be. The elections were so widely and flagrantly rigged that civil rebellion broke out in the region. When this could not be quelled by the militarised police the army was called in. Thus the political leadership of the country by this action exposed its weakness and when the military realised that political power depended on the military, some radicals within the army simply shoved the political leaders aside though *a coup d'etat* characterized by widespread bloodshed occasioning the killing of the Premier of the North, Sir Ahmadu Bello, the Federal Prime Minister, Sir Abubakar Tafawa Balewa, the Premier of the West, Chief Ladoke Akintola, Northern and Western high level military personnel such as Brigadier Maimalari, Colonel Abogo Largema, Colonel Pam, Colonel Kur Muhammad, Brigadier Adesujo Adermulegun and Colonel Ralph Shodeinde. The coup opened the Pandora box of ethnic cleansing of political and military leaders of some section of the country which later drew a response from military personnel of the North in a counter coup and widespread and blind reprisals in the North against southerners but primarily against Igbos. These events were later to precipitate a civil war between 1967 and 1970 in which more than a million people perished either directly from military action or indirectly from collateral damage of military action. The fault line in the country while not caused by elections seemed to surface at election time posing fundamental challenge to the very foundation of the country.

Revisionist commentators sometimes heap the blame of these events on the military. But in reality the military would not have intervened if not because the civilian leadership exposed its soft under belly. The military is trained in the art of violence and the only way they know how to solve differences is through the act of warfare or violence. Those who do not learn from the lesson of history are doomed to repeat it, says George Santayana. Did our politicians learn anything from these events?

When in 1979, after thirteen years of military rule, the civilians were handed over power the affliction of electoral malpractices were not cured. The old political parties came in different hues and colours but their provenance was unmistakable. The old NPC metamorphosed. into the National Party of Nigeria (NPN). The NCNC became the Nigerian Peoples Party (NPP) and the Action Group came in form of the Unity Party of Nigeria (UPN). Awolowo led the UPN while Azikiwe led the NPP and Shehu Shagari, a former parliamentary secretary under Sir Abubakar Tafawa Balewa led the NPN. The election of 1979 was almost a replay of the 1959 political drama. The NPN had the largest number of votes in the Presidential election followed by the UPN.[10]

The NPN did not quite fulfill the constitutional requirement of winning the overall number of votes and at least twenty five per cent of the votes in two-thirds of the states of the federation. It won this in twelve rather than in thirteen states out of nineteen and through legal abracadabra twelve two-thirds of states replaced the required thirteen states. The opposition protested to no end. The military in order to save its skin appeared desperate to hand over to the politicians and the military gladly accepted the legal interpretation which satisfied nobody. But this was to be a minor thing compared with what happened in 1983 when the ruling NPN threw caution to the winds and flagrantly rigged the election in a land slide in spite of the fact that the country had been run aground. The military wing of the ruling class intervened to save the situation in December 1983 and by 1984 Obafemi Awolowo withdrew from politics and issued a curse on Nigeria that the country would for a long time not enjoy democratic governance. In 1987 the old war horse died and many of his supporters vowed never to vote again in the sham elections of Nigeria.

The story is told about farmers in Ekiti going to their farms in the morning of the 1993 Presidential election. When told about the coming election, some of them innocently said they thought election had died with Awolowo in 1987! Azikwe died in 1996 having become politically irrelevant and had the misfortune of witnessing the rogueish regime of Sanni Abacha. The military that came into power in 1983 remained in the saddle to 1999 after annulling the elections of 1993 won by Moshood Abiola the Presidential candidate of the Social Democratic Party (SDP). The military under General Badamasi Babangida a suave military politician who had a large followership and loyalty because of his use of state resources to benefit his supporters, had organised two political parties, the Social Democratic Party — a party "a little to the left" and the National Republican Convention NRC — a party "a little to the right" Babangida had rightly recognised two tendencies in Nigeria's political life, one was conservatism and the other was some kind of socialist or social welfare radicalism. He therefore organized two parties to represent these tendencies. In spite of the souless origin of these two parties, they took on lives of their own and evolved into living parties which threw up two improbable Presidential candidates in the persons of M.K.O. Abiola, a multimillionaire friend of Babangida parading himself as leader of a socialist party and Bashir Tofa, a Kano multimillionaire friend of Babangida. It seems head or tail Babangida could not lose. But he apparently expected his Northern friend to win.

He miscalculated in this because Abiola's legendary generousity worked for him, to the extent that he even defeated Bashir Tofa in his own ward in Kano. The electoral umpire Professor Humphrey Nwosu seemed to have run an election that has been adjudged the fairest and most transparent Nigeria. During the election, electors filed before the symbols of their parties, voted and were counted in what was called "open-secret" ballot or "option A4." When the results showed Abiola had won, his enemies within the military threatened to kill Abiola and possibly Babangida and the elections were subsequently annulled whatever reasons were given for this were not believed by anybody and from there on it was clear that elections can never resolve the fissiparous political tendencies in the country. The military again, as a palliative, put together a contraption of unelected military civilian government headed by a former uni-lever executive Ernest Shonekan as an interim administration after President Babangida abandoned ship. This did not work and a full blast military administration headed by General Sanni Abacha, Minister of defence, shoved aside Shonekan and administered the country until 1998, when he died and a temporary administration by another military man, General Abdusalami Abubakar took over and quickly arranged power transfer to a civilian administration. Abacha's administration was the most nakedly brutal the country had ever seen. He used terror and murder to cover the corruption of his administration. This was particularly an open sore of a country in which thievery, thuggery and ethnic cleansing became state policy. The reaction from the Yoruba people who were the target was measured and effective and involved enlisting of international support through the media and international institutions like the Commonwealth and the United Nations and even the Papacy. This unfortunate situation following a fairly well conducted election was somehow resolved when Abiola the unfortunate Victor who became a victim and Abacha his tormentor died one after the other in 1998 in what appears to be unnatural deaths, although there is no evidence to support possible conspiracy involving international secret services.

The elections that were speedily organised pitching the military backed candidate of General Olusegun

Obasanjo, a former military head of state who had narrowly escaped death in Abacha's gulag because of international intervention, against Olu Falae, a former secretary to Babangida's military government, erstwhile Minister of Finance and a retired banker, predictably resulted in Obasanjo's victory. Obasanjo ran on the platform of the **Peoples Democratic Party** (PDP) an all corners party void of any ideology but "the sharing of the national cake" while Chief Olu Falae ran on the combined platform of the **Alliance for Democracy Party** which saw itself as a reincarnation of Awolowo's philosophy and the **All Nigeria Peoples Party** (ANPP). As a recurring decimal the outcome of the election was hotly disputed and Chief Olu Falae was however prevailed upon by some Yoruba leaders to let the result be in order to avoid possible military intervention to prevent Obasanjo one of their sons from taking over. Obasanjo was electorally not supported at home but he seemed to have been imposed on the country by the Northern political and military caucus. Peace however prevailed because the results of the election at state levels seemed to have reflected the wishes of the people. The President however felt politically diminished for having no home support and he appeared determined to reverse the situation in the subsequent election of 2003. He somehow cajoled the A.D state governments in the South-West to support his re-election promising to support their own re-election. He turned the tables against them by using state institutions of the army, police and intelligence organisation to rig them out of power in 2003. Only Lagos, perhaps for fear of a peoples rebellion survived the onslaught. At the national level the PDP used the same method to get out of the way the challenge of General Muhammed Buhari of the All Nigerian Peoples Party (ANPP). Obasanjo's strategy as loudly publicised was to bring the South West into the "main stream" of feasting on the national cake. The rigging machine was again cranked up when the same thing but worse still happened in 2007 when Obasanjo chose to hand over power to an apparently sick man Umaru Shehu Yar'Adua. The scandal was on such a scale that Yar'Adua the beneficiary openly stated that the election that brought him to power was faulty if not fraudulent. He went ahead to set up a commission to make recommendations about how to hold proper elections in the future. Some of the recommendations of this body included a really independent electoral commission directly funded not by the presidency but by a line — budgetary vote guaranteed by the constitution. Its chairman was also to be chosen by the National judicial council with additional support of labour and representatives of the intelligentsia and all other stake holders. Elections were also to hold with sufficient time lag to permit disposal of all electoral challenges and disputes before people were sworn into offices. Even though changes were made in the electoral laws by the PDP controlled legislature and the executive branches of government but public opinion felt the entire recommendations of the Justice Muhammad Uwais report should have been enacted into law. Suffice it to say that when Attahiru Jega, a former Vice-Chancellor of Bayero and former President of ASSU (Academic Senior Staff of University Union) was appointed as Chairman of the Independent National Electoral Commission (INEC) people were ready to give the commission whose reputation had been ruined by the incorrigibly corrupt commission led by a Professor Maurice Iwu, of despicable character and reputation, a chance. At the same time Attahiru Jega inherited virtually all the staff put in place by Maurice Iwu and people wondered how the same characters who had been involved in previously discredited elections could suddenly perform wonders.

Jega's reputation made people to wait and see. A new voter's registration was embarked upon at billions of Naira's cost and at the end of the exercise in which members of the NYSC (National Youth Service Corps) were largely used as electoral officials close to 67 million voters list was compiled. Even during registration it became obvious that fiddling with figures was indulged in by politicians who intended to use their figures to inflate results in order to ensure victory for themselves and their political parties. There were disputes over the order of elections, some wanting the Presidential poll to be first while others preferred other arrangements. The ruling party wanted the Presidential election first so that all other tiers of governments could coast in on the victory of whoever won the Presidential poll which the party in power the PDP with advantage of incumbency hoped it would win. The PDP had however been weakened by internal problems arising from the policy of zoning. The Northern wing of the party represented by Adamu Ciroma, Abubakar Atiku and even General Ibrahim Babangida had argued that the death of Umaru Yar'Adua should not deny the North its turn of eight years in the saddle of the Presidency of Nigeria. They had argued that the holding operation of Goodluck Jonathan for one year from 2010 to 2011 should give way to a Northern candidate to conclude the Northern term started by Yar'Adua in 2007. The North had even anointed Abubakar Atiku as its consensus candidate on the PDP platform. The Jonathan group which included former President Olusegun Obasanjo unconvincingly argued against the zoning principle. Jonathan using the levers of power was able to muscle in and win his party's nomination. It was however doubtful if he would be able to command the followership of members of the PDP's rank and file. In fact some of the Northern PDP leaders openly said they would make the country ungovernable. So, even before Jonathan confronted General Muhammed Buhari who had formed a new political party the Congress of Peoples Convention (CPC) after leaving his old party of All Nigerians National Party (ANPP). The country had never seen anything like the CPC before. Some commentators likened it to the religious movement that swept Usman Dan Fodio and his Islamic reformers into power in what later became

Northern Nigeria in the 19th Century. Muhammad Buhari attracted all those who for one reason or the other were disenchanted or disillusioned with the situation of Nigeria. The increasing level of poverty and immiseration particularly in the North turned a political party into a quasi social and religious movement. There was open and in some cases clandestine embrace of Muhammad Buhari as the Muslim and Northern candidate. This was to be the candidate's undoing nationally. Many people in the South saw him as a Northern hegemonist and a Muslim fanatic, but ironically Buhari was embraced either openly or secretly by the Southern intelligentsia who felt that the problems of the country were so immense and complex that only a man of Buhari's moral fibre could successfully tackle them. Buhari's lean purse did not allow him to have an effective structure on the ground in the country or to mount a sustained media and political campaign as was apparently done by Jonathan who used State organs, particularly the media, intelligence organisation as well as police and transportation infrastructure especially the Presidential aviation fleet to outwit his opponent.

The Independent electoral commission naturally had to rely on government support for its own transportation of electoral materials and personnel all over the country. The deployment of the NYSC as *ad hoc* electoral staff and the use of university officials as returning officers to a certain extent, at least on the surface gave credibility to the electoral process. The decision of INEC to overrule the National Security Adviser (NSA) that voters should leave immediately after voting rather than waiting to see votes counted at each polling booth gave some semblance of confidence to cynics and doubters. When the election proper began with the National Assembly elections there was a hitch and seeming unpreparedness hut this was overcome as time went on after some adjustments. The Presidential elections which had been eagerly awaited was conducted with more surefootedness by INEC after the tardiness, prevarication and slothfulness characteristic of the National Assembly election. The Presidential Poll was won by Goodluck Jonathan the incumbent President who easily won more than required 25% of the votes in two-thirds of the States of the federation.[11]

He was massively supported in the South-South minority areas and also in the North-central minority areas and in the South East and at least won twenty five percent of the votes in most of the States in the South-West including Osun State where the candidate of the ACN Ribadu carried the State. He also won 25% of the votes in Kaduna, Adamawa, Sokoto and Taraba in the North. The level of apparent victory was impressive but there were doubts about the percentages of electoral victory in the South-South and South-East where returns in some States outstripped the number of registered voters or attained over ninety per cent of registered voters which was rather unusual in the global pattern of elections. There were of course widespread under-age voters in many parts of the country particularly in the North where Muhammad

Buhari won. The victory of the President occasioned some form of rebellion when violence broke out all over the North leading to widespread, bombing, arson, murder, including the killing of electoral officers and thirteen NYSC members in Bauchi and even attempted attacks on palaces of Emirs of Sokoto and Zaria. This unprecedented violence took the Security Agencies by surprise even though ordinary laymen knew that Nigeria was really sitting on a tight rope and that the country was bound to violence no matter who won the Presidential election. If Buhari had won there would have been violence in the Niger-Delta just as violence occurred in the North. The question then was whether the violence was spontaneous on sponsored. There are reasons to suggest that it was both. There is no doubt that expectations were so high on both sides that the loser was bound to become so sore that if violence occurred he would welcome it if only to teach the opponent a lesson. Religious sentiments crept into the elections following on one hand the seeming endorsement of Jonathan by the Pentecostal movement while Muslims on the other hand generally supported Buhari. Religious sentiments were easily exploited and they quickly boiled into violence. It        is now clear through the privilege of hindsight that money played a major role in the election and many members of the NYSC were forced against their will  to dance  to  the  tune of local political   barons   who    threatened, bribed, beat or cajoled them to do their will. The violence which followed the Presidential poll allowed the PDP in the North to regroup and to return candidates of the unperforming party into power. In many of the States the dominant political tendencies were respected. The Action Congress of Nigeria (ACN) sacked the PDP in the South-West and Edo State while the APGA in the South East won in Anambra and Imo while the PDP returned to power in Ebonyi, Enugu and Abia States and most the States in the South- South.

The results of the Presidential election were rejected by the CPC and by General Buhari who had indicated that he would not go to any law court to challenge the result. This made many to feel that his position gave vent to the street action in the North. Buhari however said he would not stop his party from going to courts. It is however unlikely that any court would reverse the electoral victory of a sitting President in Nigeria. The inability of the opposition to unite due to the puritanical rigidity and absolute lack of realism of General Muhammad Buhari of the CPC and the vaunting ambition of some of the leaders of the ACN among other reasons opened the door wide for President Jonathan's relatively easy victory. If the two parity leaders had sacrificed personal interests for the overall determination to remove the PDP as they publicly vowed to do, the result of the election may have been different. As long as the opposition remains hopelessly divided and inclined to run different shows so will the much derided and despised PDP continue to dominate the political arena irrespective of it performance and the country will inch gradually towards one party state which has failed in many parts of the world. The onus to help Nigeria practice democracy lies on the leaders of the opposition as well as the ruling party. The country however has never been as divided as it is today; and this dangerous disquiet has manifested itself particularly in the North where the endemic corruption in the States has created a state of insurrection in Bauchi, Gombe and Borno, Plateau and even in Kaduna Slates with the result that there is general insecurity in the North and even all over the country. Elections rather than unify this country or provide peaceful change- of government have rather exacerbated the fundamental division in the country.

In spite of this, the 2011 elections have been adjudged to be generally fair by informed observers both locally and internationally. The United States for example applauded the 2011 elections as being better than 2007 election but expressed serious concerns about reports of alleged ballot box snatching and stuffing. A retired government official from the North of the country observed

> *"...Given our unenviable history of electoral misconduct spanning over the last 50 years, INEC under Prof Attahiru Jega's leadership can be said to have come out well in spite of the odds and the brief period of public skepticism occasioned by the*

*commission's initial tottering steps and seeming self doubt....*

*Relative to the 2003 and 2007 election, the 2011 election was more transparent as it generally reflected the votes openly cast, counted and recorded in the various polling booths. Many of the complaints centred around what transpired at the collation centres, where the voters appeared to have been shut out from defending their votes as much as they did at the polling booths.*

*"... The overall verdict remains, however that in the 2011 election we have moved positively forward in our quest for electoral excellence, although we need to refine our methods to, make it transparent through and through...."*[12]

Writing on the same issue a retired senior academic wrote

*"... The 2011 elections...represent the beginning of a process which one hopes will culminate in the people choosing without much fuss or hassle those who will rule them. In this regard, the relative impartiality that attended the conduct of the polls, in which, for once, the electoral commission chairman appeared to have been truly independent of the ruling or any other party or interest, is welcome development. All the same, it has to be quickly added that in Nigeria. . . incumbent rulers and their parties enjoy fir too many privileges and*

*advantages vis a vis the opposition for elections to be truly fair. The political structure is also subject to the many deformities and inequalities to permit of equal opportunity of access to power.*

*There were malpractices at all levels of the balloting process — bribing of INEC auxiliary staff to engage in multiple ballot — thumb printing, purchase of votes on voting queues, intimidation of opposition party agents at collation centres, some of the worst cases of electoral irregularities would appear to have taken place in PDP strongholds in Eastern Nigeria, in the Niger-Delta and in parts of Northern Nigeria. In Eastern Nigeria and the Niger-Delta for example PDP scores range between 97.67 and 99.63 per cent of the votes cast in Presidential polls. These are figures that are not replicated anywhere else in the country, they also defy all statistical analyses based on voter registration, turn out of voters, or the factor of candidates' home constituency.* "[13]

What was obvious was that Goodluck Jonathan was personally preferred to the dour and ascetic general. In other words people voted for Jonathan rather than the PDP and hoped that the newly returned President will in his policies transcend his party, Whether this is a forlorn hope lies in the pregnant future.

What is to be done and what is at the bottom of electoral heist in1 Nigeria? Why is it almost impossible to hold elections that losers can accept without resort to the courts or the streets of protest. In the last fifty years we have not had any election that was not a subject of disputation and challenge and rather for the situation to improve, it is getting worse. One of the reasons is the structural imbalance in the country in which political power for long was located in one part of the country to the detriment of free access to power by others no matter how qualified or talented they may be. Some people have advocated everybody belonging to the "mainstream". This would amount to having a one party state in which electoral disputes will be resolved at party level. Apart from being anachronistic, one party States tend to collapse if there is no avenue for alternative views. This was the case in the Soviet Union and Yugoslavia. The recent dispute over zoning within the PDP occasioning regional animosity is also a point undermining advocacy for one party state. In the case of Nigeria there is need for reducing the power in the centre so that controlling the centre will not be a matter of political and economic life or death as it is presently. Weakening the centre would not automatically mean free elections at state level but events in Kano and the South West the two areas of political sophistication proves that the local people can vote in or remove parties if the electoral umpire is fair. There is also too much reliance on force and money in our elections with little or no emphasis of party platforms and ideology. Elections have become investments and like any business, people take risks with the hope of reaping bountiful dividends. In the distributive system of governments that we run with little emphasis on production but all the emphasis on sharing what essentially is the bounty of nature, no consideration whatsoever is placed on honesty, probity and integrity. If the State had not been turned into a commissioned agent skimming off profits from multinational oil corporations, the bitterness witnessed in recent times will not be there. In other words there is need to de-emphacise this distributive and sharing aspect of governance in favour of production. The time may indeed have come for fiscal federalism and resource control so that Nigerians can go back to work instead of politics becoming the quickest means of individual riches, wealth and status.

Elections since 1951 to the present have not been able to foster a    feeling of common destiny and if we are to remain together we must find ways and means to harmonise individual and group rights within an overarching federal architecture. But the key to the removal of this curse of election lies in education, adoption of full proof    technological electoral machinery to minimise tampering with the electoral process. We must also build a Nigerian economy in which people who wish to work would have work to do and in which politics will be a vocation rather than a profession. This was what it was in the past and we must go back to the past in order to guarantee our future. Dissolution of the federation will not guarantee fair election in the successor States. This is the experience and verdict of history. The chaos in Somalia proves that common ethnic and religious identity is not a guarantee of stability, security, democracy and free elections. What is necessary is political restructuring of the country so as to have States, perhaps based on present six zones, which are viable and sustainable and deemphacising the centre so that political struggle and electoral contestation will be localised instead of the current struggle of seizure of the centre by all and every means possible including rigging of elections or through a military *putsch* or coup *d'etat*.

## Notes

1. The Lagos Standard August 11, 1915 in Akinjide Osuntokun "The Genesis of Lagos paramountcy in the rise of Nigerian nationalism" 15th Convocation Lecture, Lagos State University Press, 2008.
2. Margery Perham Lugard. *The Years of Authority*, 1898— 1945; The Maker *of Modern Nigeria*, Collins, London, 1960.
3. *Weekly Record* 5. Oct., 1918.
4. James Coleman: *Nigeria Background to Nationalism*, University of California Press Berkely and Los Angeles 1965, p.153.
5. Coleman *ibid*, p.264.

6. Joseph Oduola Osuntokun. My *View of the Coin*: A *Participant's Account of the Politics of the First Republic*, CCC.

7. Books, Ibadan, 2003.

8. Coleman *op cit*, p. 361.

9. see Akinjide Osuntokun Chief S.L.A. *Akintola: His Life and Times*; Frank Cass, London, 1982

10. 1979 Poll Result

| GNPP | UPN | NPN | NPP | PRP |
|---|---|---|---|---|
| 1,841,192 | 3,040,006 | 4,277,756 | 2,1333,867 | 1,238,412 |
| 1,4.69% | 24.25% | 34.13% | 17.02% | 9.8% |

11. 39,469,484 people voted. Parties were voted for as follows:

ACN        -        2,079,151 (5.42%)

ANPP       -        917,012(2.40%)

CPC        -        12,214,853(31.98%)

PDP        -        22,495,187 (58.89%)

12. "Bukar Usman retired Federal Permanent Secretary" in the *Guardian* Monday July 18, 2011.

13. Dr. G.A. Akinola *The Guardian* July 3, 2011.

## Select Bibliography

1. AMADU KURFI: The Nigerian General Elections 1959 and 1979 and the Aftermath, Macmillan Nigeria Publishers Ilupeju, 1983.

2. H.N. Nwosu: *Laying the Foundation for Nigeria's Democracy: My Account of June 12, 1993 Presidential elections and its annulment*, Macmillan Nigeria Publishers Ilupeju, 2008

3. James S. Coleman: Nigeria: *Background to Nationalism*, University of California Press Berkeley and Los Angeles, 1965.

4. Oyin Ogunba ed.: *Governance and the Electoral Process: Nigeria and the United States*, ASAN Lagos, 1997.

5. Alan Burns: *History of Nigeria*, George Allen and Unwin Ltd, London, 1948.

6. Thomas Hodgkin: *Nationalism in* Colonial Africa, Lcr ldh, Muller, 1959.

7. C.R. Niven: *How Nigeria is Governed*, London Longmans, 1950.

8. Margery Perham: *Lugard; The Years of Authority*, The Maker of Modern 1898-1945: Nigeria London Collins, 1960.

9.    Obafemi Awolowo: *Path to Nigerian Freedom*, London Faber, 1947.

10.   Nnamdi Azikiwe: *My Odyssey*: An Autobiography C. Hurst London, 1970.

11.   Ahmadu Bello: *My Life*, Cambridge University Press, 1962.

12.   Joseph Oduola Osuntokun: *My view of the Coin*: *A Participants Account of the Politics of the First Republic,* CCC Press Ibadan. 2003.

13.   Obafemi Awolowo: *Awo: Autobiography of Chief Obafemi Awolowo.* Cambridge University Press, 1960.

14.   Akinjide Osuntokun: *The Life and Times of Chief S.L.A. Akintola.* Frank Cass, London, 1978.

15.   Akinjide Osuntokun: *The Genesis of Lagos' Paramountcy in the Rise of Nigerian Nationalism,* 15th Convocation Lecture, Lagos State University, 2008.

16.   Akinjide Osuntokun: Power Broker: *The Life and Times of Sir Kashim Ibrahim.* Spectrum Books, Ibadan, 1984.

17. Adegoke Adelabu: *Africa in Ebullition*. Ibadan, 1952.

18. Ladipo Adamolekun ed.: *Ideas for Development.* Caligata Publishing Company Ltd., Ibadan, 2011.

19. Kenneth Post & Jenkins George: *The Price of Liberty*: *Personality and Politics in Colonial Nigeria*: Cambridge University Press, 1973.

20. Richard Skiar: *Nigerian Political Parties*: *Power in an Emergent African Nation*: Princeton University Press. Princeton N.J., 1963.

21. Sir William Neville Geary: *Nigeria Under British Rule*. Methuen & Co. London, 1927.

22. Insa Nolte: *Obafemi Awolowo and the Making of Remo*. College Press, Ibadan, 2011.